The Art of Procuring
Pleasant Dreams

ANOTHER MEANS OF

PRESERVING *health*

TO BE ATTENDED TO

IS THE HAVING A

CONSTANT SUPPLY OF

FRESH *air* IN YOUR

bedchamber.

Benjamin Franklin

THE ART OF
PROCURING PLEASANT
Dreams

AMERICAN ROOTS

Applewood Books
CARLISLE, MASSACHUSETTS

The short works Applewood offers in its American Roots series have been selected to connect us. The books are tactile mementos of American passions by some of America's most famous writers. Each of these has meant something very personal to me.

Both my wife's family and my own have Philadelphia roots. My grandfather-in-law was president for a time of the Franklin Institute. His Philadelphia home had a sleeping porch. There, he would sleep, even on the coldest winter nights in the open air under blankets. It is no wonder this sleep habit has been passed down through the family to my wife, who, like her grandfather, needs her sleep to be surrounded by the fresh air of any season.

> "*Another means of preserving health to be attended to is the having a constant supply of fresh air in your bedchamber.*"

᧞Phil Zuckerman
PUBLISHER

As a great part of our life is spent in sleep, during which we have sometimes pleasant and sometimes painful dreams, it becomes of some consequence to obtain the one kind and avoid the other; for whether real or imaginary, pain is pain and pleasure is pleasure. If we can sleep without dreaming, it is well that painful dreams are avoided. If, while we sleep, we can have any pleasant dreams, it is, as the

French say, autant de gagné, so much added to the pleasure of life.

To this end it is, in the first place, necessary to be careful in preserving health by due exercise and great temperance; for in sickness the imagination is disturbed, and disagreeable, sometimes terrible, ideas are apt to present themselves. Exercise should precede meals, not immediately follow them; the first promotes, the latter, unless moderate, obstructs digestion. If, after exercise, we feed sparingly, the digestion will be easy and good, the body lightsome, the temper cheerful, and all the animal functions performed agreeably. Sleep, when it follows, will be natural and undisturbed, while indolence, with full feeding, occasions nightmares and horrors inexpressible; we fall from precipices, are assaulted by wild beasts, murderers, and demons, and experience every variety of distress. Observe, however, that the quantities of food and exercise are relative things: those who move much may, and indeed ought to, eat more; those who use little exercise should eat little. In general, mankind, since the improvement of cookery, eat about twice as much as nature requires. Suppers are not bad if we have not dined; but restless nights follow hearty suppers after full dinners. Indeed, as there is a difference in constitutions, some rest well after these meals; it costs them only a frightful dream and an apoplexy, after which they sleep till doomsday. Nothing is more common in the newspapers than instances of people who, after eating a hearty supper, are found dead abed in the morning.

Another means of preserving health to be attended to is the having a constant supply of fresh air in your bedchamber. It has been a great mistake, the sleeping in rooms exactly closed and the beds surrounded by curtains.

No outward air that may come in to you is so unwholesome as the unchanged air, often breathed, of a close chamber. As boiling water does not grow hotter by long boiling if the particles that receive greater heat can escape, so living bodies do not putrefy if the particles, so fast as they become putrid, can be thrown off. Nature expels them by the pores of the skin and lungs, and in a free, open air they are carried off; but in a close room we receive them again and again, though they become more and more corrupt. A number of persons crowded into a small room thus spoil the air in a few minutes, and even render it mortal as the Black Hole at Calcutta. A single person is said to spoil only a gallon of air per minute, and therefore requires a longer time to spoil a chamberful; but it is done, however, in proportion, and many putrid disorders hence have their origin. It is recorded of Methuselah, who, being the longest liver, may be supposed to have best preserved his health, that he slept always in the open air; for when he had lived five hundred years an angel said to him: "Arise, Methuselah, and build thee an house, for thou shalt live yet five hundred years longer." But Methuselah answered and said: "If I am to live but five hundred years longer, it is not worth while to build me an house; I will sleep in the air, as I have been used to do." Physicians, after having for ages contended that the sick should not be indulged with fresh air, have at length discovered that it may do them good. It is therefore to be hoped that they may in time discover likewise that it is not hurtful to those who are in health, and that we may then be cured of the aerophobia that at present distresses weak minds, and makes them choose to be stifled and poisoned rather than leave open the window of a bedchamber or put down the glass of a coach.

Confined air, when saturated with perspirable matter, will not receive more, and that matter must remain in our bodies and occasion diseases; but it gives us some previous notice of its being about to be hurtful by producing certain uneasiness, slight indeed at first, such as with regard to the lungs is a trifling sensation and to the pores of the skin a kind of restlessness which is difficult to describe, and few that feel it know the cause of it. But we may recollect that sometimes, on waking in the night, we have, if

warmly covered, found it difficult to get asleep again. We turn
often, without finding repose in
any position. This fidgetiness (to
use a vulgar expression for want
of a better) is occasioned wholly
by uneasiness in the skin, owing
to the retention of the perspirable
matter, the bedclothes having
received their quantity, and being
saturated, refusing to take any
more. To become sensible of this
by an experiment, let a person keep
his position in the bed, throw off
the bedclothes, and suffer fresh air
to approach the part uncovered
of his body; he will then feel that
part suddenly refreshed, for the

air will immediately relieve the skin by receiving, licking up, and carrying off the load of perspirable matter that approaches the warm skin, in receiving its part of that vapor, receives therewith a degree of heat that rarefies and renders it lighter, by cooler and therefore heavier fresh air, which for a moment supplies its place, and then, being likewise changed and warmed, gives way to a succeeding quantity.

This is the order of nature to prevent animals being infected by their own perspiration. He will now be sensible of the difference between the part exposed to the air and that which, remaining sunk in the bed, denies the air access; for this part now manifests its uneasiness more distinctly by the comparison, and the seat of the uneasiness is more plainly perceived than when the whole surface of the body was affected by it.

Here, then, is one great and general cause of unpleasing dreams. For when the body is uneasy the mind will be disturbed by it, and disagreeable ideas of various kinds will in sleep be the natural consequences. The remedies, preventive and curative, follow.

1. By eating moderately (as before advised for health's sake)

less perspirable matter is produced in a given time; hence the bedclothes receive it longer before they are saturated, and we may therefore sleep longer before we are made uneasy by their refusing to receive any more.

2. By using thinner and more porous bedclothes, which will suffer the perspirable matter more easily to pass through them, we are less incommoded, such being longer tolerable.

3. When you are awakened by this uneasiness and find you cannot easily sleep again, get out of bed, beat up and turn your pillow, shake the bedclothes well, with at least

twenty shakes, then throw the bed open and leave it to cool; in the mean while, continuing undressed, walk about your chamber till your skin has had time to discharge its load, which it will do sooner as the air may be dryer and colder. When you begin to feel the cold air unpleasant, then return to your bed and you will soon fall asleep, and your sleep will be sweet and pleasant. All the scenes presented to your fancy will be, too, of a pleasing kind. I am often as agreeably entertained with them as by the scenery of an opera. If you happen to be too indolent to get out of bed, you may, instead of it, lift up your bedclothes with one arm and leg, so as to draw in a good deal of fresh air, and by letting them fall force it out again. This, repeated twenty times, will so clear them of the perspirable matter they have imbibed as to permit your sleeping well for some time afterward. But this latter method is not equal to the former.

Those who do not love trouble and can afford to have two beds will find great luxury in rising, when they wake in a hot bed, and going into the cool one. Such shifting of beds would also be of great service to persons ill of a fever, as it refreshes and frequently procures sleep. A very large bed that will admit a removal so distant from the first situation as to be cool and sweet may in a degree answer the same end.

One or two observations more will conclude this little piece. Care must be taken, when you lie down, to dispose your pillow so as to suit your manner of placing your head and to be perfectly easy; then place your limbs so as not to bear inconveniently hard upon one another, as, for instance, the joints of your ankles; for though a bad position may at first give but little pain and be hardly noticed, yet a continuance will render it less tolerable, and the uneasiness may come on while you are asleep and disturb your imagination. These are the rules of the art. But though they will generally prove effectual in producing the end intended, there is a case in which the most punctual observance of them will be totally fruitless. I need not mention the case to you, my dear friend; but my account of the art would be imperfect without it. The case is when the person who desires to have pleasant dreams has not taken care to preserve, what is necessary above all things, A GOOD CONSCIENCE.